EDITOR: MARTIN WINDROW

OSPREY
MILITARY

MEN-AT-ARM

CANADIAN C
1860·

Text by
DAVID ROSS
MILITARY CURATOR, PARKS, CANADA

and
GRANT TYLER
CURATOR, MILITARY HISTORY SOCIETY OF MANITOBA

Colour plates by
RICK SCOLLINS

Published in 1992 by
Osprey Publishing Ltd
59 Grosvenor Street, London W1X 9DA
© Copyright 1992 Osprey Publishing Ltd

ISBN 1 85532 226 9

Filmset in Great Britain
Printed through Bookbuilders Ltd, Hong Kong

Artist's Note

Readers may care to note that the original paintings
from which the colour plates in this book were
prepared are available for private sale. All
reproduction copyright whatsoever is retained by the
publisher. All enquiries should be addressed to:

Richard Scollins
14 Ladywood Road,
Ilkeston,
Derbyshire

The publishers regret that they can enter into no
correspondence upon this matter.

For a catalogue of all books published by Osprey Military
please write to:

The Marketing Manager,
Consumer Catalogue Department,
Osprey Publishing Ltd,
Michelin House, 81 Fulham Road,
London SW3 6RB

Acknowledgements

Many of the contemporary photographs in this book
are the work of William Notman (1826–91), whose
photographs are preserved in the Notman
Photographic Collection in the McCord Museum at
McGill University. The help and encouragement of
Mr Stanley Triggs, Curator of the Collection, is
gratefully acknowledged.

Like so many students of Canadian and British
uniforms the writers have long benefited from the
encyclopaedic knowledge and generosity of Mr W. Y.
Carman, the doyen of British military uniform
authorities. Special thanks are also due to Karen Tyler
for her invaluable help in preparing the manuscript.
We would also like to thank the following for their
assistance, which took varied forms: René Chartrand,
Paul Fortier, Howard Garrett, Jack Summers and
Malcolm Wake.

Author's note

The aim of this book is to outline the sequence of
military events in Canada in the 1860s—the large
British Army presence, due to the tensions caused by
the US Civil War; the Fenian Raids of 1866 and 1870;
and the Red River Expedition—and to illustrate some
of the uniforms of the Canadian Volunteer Militia and
the British Army, in particular examples of winter
dress required by the severe Canadian climate, and the
uniforms worn by staff officers. Fortunately for
historians of dress, soldiers of this era were
enthusiastic patrons of the Montreal photographer
William Notman, whose surviving records include
many glass negatives and his print books containing
copies of every portrait he took. This treasure trove of
military and civilian costume is preserved and
maintained by the McCord Museum in Montreal. Its
value to the history of dress in Canada is incalculable.

THE CANADIAN MILITIA 1840–1860

The union of Upper and Lower Canada[1] in 1841 resulted in a combined Sedentary Militia of some 426 battalions, totalling 250,000 men—a considerable force even by today's standards. This was, however, a paper army, based upon universal service; and the battalions, which mustered annually for only one day, were really only intended for mobilization purposes. The annual muster was a sight to behold:

'Here there was no uniformity attempted of dress, of appearance, of movement; a few had coats, others jackets; a greater number had neither coats nor jackets, but appeared in their shirt sleeves, white or checked, or clean or dirty, in edifying variety! Some wore hats, others caps, others their own shaggy heads of hair. Some had firelocks, some had old swords suspended in belts, or stuck in their waist bands; but the greater number shouldered sticks or umbrellas.'[2]

This less than ideal situation prompted some of the more patriotic, military-minded citizens to form volunteer corps, which, as they received no government support, provided their own uniforms and equipment.

The Militia Act of 1846 did little to change the situation that had existed since union. Men between 18 and 60 were still liable to be called out, divided into two classes: the first class, who would be called

[1] The Province of Canada, a British North American colony comprising Canada West (Ontario) and Canada East (Quebec), resulted from the union of Upper and Lower Canada in 1841.
[2] G. F. G. Stanley, *Canada's Soldiers*, p. 210.

Major S. J. Lyman, Montreal Garrison Artillery, 1864, in full dress. Dark blue tunic and trousers with scarlet collar and cuffs, as for the Royal Artillery, but with silver lace, braid, belts and buttons: a good example of how closely Canadians followed British regulations. The cost alone of such uniforms helped to ensure that officers came from the upper economic, as well as social strata of the community. (Notman Collection)

upon first in an emergency, comprised 18 to 40 year olds; the second class, 40 to 60 year olds. The Act also provided for an emergency force of up to 30,000 men to be found from the Sedentary Militia through voluntary enlistment, or ballot in the event that quotas were not met. The militia was administered by the Adjutant General, assisted by two Assistant Adjutants General: E. P. Tache for Canada East and Alan McNab for Canada West. The Governor General was empowered to authorize formation of volunteer cavalry, artillery and infantry corps which, as in the past, were required to organize and finance themselves. This, however, was the first official recognition given to the volunteer principle in Canada.

Needless to say, Canada was almost wholly dependent upon British regular troops for her defence: a responsibility the home government was less and less inclined to accept. Cost was a factor, but so too was the belief that greater political freedom went hand-in-hand with the responsibility for one's own defence.

With the outbreak of the Crimean War in March 1854 Great Britain was obliged to draw upon her colonial garrisons. By October all British regulars except the 16th Regt., the Royal Canadian Rifle Regiment and two companies of Royal Artillery had been ordered from Canada. This left only 1,695 regulars to garrison the entire province. Faced with this rather grim situation, and the possibility that the

Commanding Officers of the Montreal Active Volunteer Force, 1860, in full dress uniform. L to R: Lt. Col. R. S. Tylee, CO Battalion of Montreal Volunteer Artillery since 1857; Lt. Col. H. H. Whitney, CO Montreal Light Infantry since 1859; Major Henry Hogan, CO Field Battery and Company Foot Artillery; Col. John Dyde, Commandant Volunteer Force since 1856 (ADC to the Queen 1878); Lt. Col. Thomas Wiley, CO 1st Prince of Wales' Rifles; Major George Smith, Assistant Adjutant General; Lt. Col. Elzear David, Commanding Montreal Volunteer Cavalry. All wear correct British pattern uniforms with some interesting variations; Whitney has a whip sash looped up to the fourth button of his tunic, Hogan's fur cap is unusual, and Smith, although AAG, wears the Staff Tunic of a Military Secretary. (Notman Collection)

Americans might take advantage of British preoccupation in the Crimea, the Governor General, Sir Edmund Waker Head, appointed the Adjutant General, Col. Frederick de Rottenburg, head of a committee tasked with investigating the state of the militia and its reorganization.

The resulting Militia Act of 1855 contained several important provisions. The Governor General was to be Commander-in-Chief of the militia. The Province was divided into 18 military districts (nine each in Canada East and West) each commanded by an Assistant Adjutant General with the rank of colonel, and assisted by a small staff, all of whom were unpaid. While retaining the Sedentary Militia, the Act also provided for an 'Active Militia' (later called Class A) of not more than 5,000 volunteers which would be armed, equipped, trained and paid by the Government. The new volunteers received ten days' training per year (20 in the artillery), and privates were paid at a rate of five shillings per day.[1]

An establishment of 16 troops of cavalry, seven field batteries, five companies of artillery, 50 companies of rifles and a provincial marine was initially authorized. It is from this volunteer force that the present Canadian Militia traces its descent. In essence, the Act provided for a cadre of trained, armed volunteers who could be called upon to maintain internal security in the absence of British regulars.

The new volunteer force found such great popularity that by 1856 additional units were authorized. These units, known as Class B, were armed, equipped and trained, but not paid.

The dress of the Volunteer Militia is described in Militia General Orders, Quebec, 16 August 1855: 'The coats of the Cavalry to be blue ... That for the Field Batteries and Foot Companies of Artillery to be blue ... That for Rifle Companies to be green ... That the coats be of tunic shape such as is now prescribed for Her Majesty's Forces' (i.e. 1854 pattern). The colour of the facings was left to the individual units. Rifles normally adopted red, black or scarlet; artillery, red or scarlet; and cavalry, white or buff. Lace was to be of silver except for artillery and rifles. A further order dated HQ Toronto, 7 February 1856, described the dress of the Sedentary

Quilted pattern shako of a junior officer of the Royal Light Infantry of Montreal (5th Volunteer Militia Rifles), 1862. This shako was in use in the British Army 1861–69. Body of dark blue wool fabric with quilt pattern stitching, patent leather peak and band, silver badge with a gilt stringed bugle. The 5th Royals are the direct ancestors of the Black Watch (Royal Highlanders) of Canada. (Donald M. Stewart Museum Collection)

Militia as the same as the uniform worn by officers of infantry of the line in the regular forces but with lace and buttons of silver.

In 1855 the Governor-General's Commission went to England and purchased arms for the Militia. These consisted of 2,500 Enfield rifled muskets, pattern 1853 long; 250 Enfield artillery carbines; 800 Colt Navy revolvers, model 1851; and 800 cavalry swords, pattern 1853. Arms and accoutrements as described in 1856 were as follows: 'Volunteer Rifleman—a rifle musket with rammer, bayonet and scabbard complete; forty round pouch, pouch belt, waist belt and gun sling, one muzzle stopper, one nipple wrench. Volunteer Cavalry Trooper—one cavalry sword with scabbard complete; one six-shooting Colt's pistol, one sword belt, one cartouche box and belt, one holster, one cleaning rod, one nipple wrench. Volunteer in Foot Company of

[1] The pay of British Infantry privates at this time amounted to only one shilling a day before stoppages.

Artillery—one rifled artillery carbine with rammer, sword bayonet and steel scabbard complete, one twenty round pouch with waist belt.'

The Indian Mutiny of 1857 engendered widespread Canadian support for Great Britain. This led the British Government to revive a plan to raise, in Canada, a regiment of regulars for British service. In the past, locally raised units had achieved regular status but these had never been intended to serve outside the country. The new regiment, the 100th Royal Canadian Regiment of Foot (gazetted in early 1858), marked the first instance of a British regular regiment being raised in Canada for service overseas. Col. de Rottenburg, Adjutant General of Militia, was given command, and within three months the regiment was up to its full strength of 1,027, the majority coming from Canada West; Canada East provided a quota of 110.

In late 1858 the 100th Regiment sailed to England dressed, for want of proper uniform, in obsolete coatees which had been stored in the Quebec Citadel for years. These were soon replaced by the regulation 1856 pattern uniform on arrival at Shorncliffe. Eventually recruiting in Canada ceased and the regiment lost its Canadian identity in all but name. The 100th became the Prince of Wales' Leinster Regiment (Royal Canadians), and was disbanded in 1922.

(It is of interest to note that Lt. Alexander R. Dunn, 11th Hussars, played an important part in recruiting the 100th Regiment. Dunn, a native of Toronto, charged with the Light Brigade at Balaclava, and his bravery in this action resulted in the first award of the Victoria Cross to a Canadian. Dunn was gazetted a major in the 100th Regiment and appointed second-in-command. By the age of 27 he had succeeded Col. de Rottenburg as commanding officer.)

Mr Stephenson, 3rd Battalion, Volunteer Militia Rifles of Canada (later 3rd Victoria Rifles), Montreal, 1861. An early winter uniform: this grey coat with grey Persian lamb fur and black braid was discarded shortly after this date. The pouch belt furnishings were also modified, a maple leaf replaced the upper roundel, and a crowned Maltese cross badge added. (Notman Collection)

THE AMERICAN CIVIL WAR

In 1859 the first battalion-strength active militia unit was formed; this was the 1st Battalion Volunteer Militia Rifles of Canada (later the Canadian Grenadier Guards). During the Civil War years several more battalions were formed, often by combining independent companies under a battalion headquarters.

Dress was described in Militia Circular Letter, Adjutant General's Office Active Force, Quebec, dated 19 May 1860, as follows: 'Field Batteries and Foot companies of Artillery, blue tunics and trousers the same as the Royal Artillery.

'Cavalry. Blue tunics, single breasted, with scarlet facings and white cord. Blue trousers with white stripes down the legs (officers to wear silver lace).

'Rifle Corps or Companies, rifle green tunics, single breasted, with scarlet facings and black cord shoulder strap; collar and cuffs slightly braided.

'Rifle green trousers with two stripes of black braid on a scarlet stripe down the leg. The Highland Companies are recommended to wear tunics, or jackets, and trews the same as those used in the regular service, the material and facings of the tunic or jacket to be in uniform with the other rifle corps.

'The buttons of the tunics of each arm of the force to be of the same description as those worn in the regular service, encircled with the words, "Volunteer Militia Canada".

Headdress. His Excellency is pleased to leave the description of the future headdress to be decided by the force themselves; but, with a view to uniformity at each station, it must be so arranged that each arm of the service will always appear on parade with the same style of headdress. The Highland Companies, however, will continue to wear headdress as may be considered most suitable to themselves.'

Strict adherence to regulation, however, was not always the case: we find several of the rifle companies clothed in varying shades of grey and brown, and some of the cavalry troops continuing to wear their white or buff facings.

April 1861 found the United States and the Southern Confederacy embroiled in bitter civil war.

Private, 1st Provisional Battalion, c.1865. Scarlet full dress tunic with dark blue collar and shoulder straps; white piping and white metal buttons, probably Canada Militia pattern with a beaver within a wreath of maple leaves. A good, clear view of the Kilmarnock cap, dark blue with a scarlet band, patent leather chin strap and white metal numeral; this was the standard other ranks' headgear at this period.

It was Lt. Col. Grant Wolseley's opinion that '. . . if the Yankees are worth their salt they will at once make peace with the South and pour 100,000 men into Canada where they can easily compensate themselves for their loss of the Confederate states, and England be perfectly unable to prevent it'. Sir William Fenwick Williams, Commander of the British Forces in North America, took action to have regular reinforcements sent to the colony.

The *Trent* and mobilization

On 8 November 1861 Capt. Charles Wilkes, USN, of the USS *San Jacinto*, seized from the British mail packet *Trent* Jefferson Davies' commissioners to England and France. The commissioners, James Mason and John Slidell, were two of the South's most prominent leaders. Wilkes arrived home to a hero's welcome. The South became optimistic of British

Ensign James Thompson of the 6th Hochelaga Light Infantry, which was raised in 1862 following the Trent *affair. He was photographed by Notman the same year. It is unusual, if not unique, to see the 1854 pattern double-breasted tunic (discarded 1857) at this late date in a newly raised unit. The tunic is scarlet with dark blue collar and cuffs, silver lace and buttons; crimson shoulder strap and sash, glazed white belt and slings. Note stud on scabbard of the 1822 pattern sword, the outdated sword knot, and the tweed trousers.*

intervention, and not without reason: when the news arrived in London on 27 November the public were incensed. For a short while war seemed imminent, with Canada as the obvious battlefield. The Canadian Volunteer Militia began to mobilize.

On 30 November Lord Russell sent to the Prince Consort, Prince Albert, copies of the British Cabinet's proposed despatches to Washington. The Prince's intervention effectively toned down the British response, making it more palatable to the Americans, and provided an opportunity for continued peace. On Christmas Day President Lincoln met with his cabinet and agreed to free the prisoners. The crisis had passed.

In the meantime Col. Daniel Lysons was sent to Canada with orders to reorganize the militia. He was accompanied by Col. Kenneth Douglas Mackenzie (Quarter Master General), Lt. Col. Garnet Joseph Wolseley (Assistant Quartermaster General), and a number of field officers and sergeant instructors.

With the country still in a state of uncertainty reinforcements continued to pour in. As the St. Lawrence River was frozen, troops were transported to Halifax, Nova Scotia, and St. John, New Brunswick. Troops previously on service at Halifax were then transported to St. Andrews, New Brunswick, and from there by rail to Canterbery; then via Woodstock to Riviére du Loupe, Canada East, in sleighs. The men travelled eight to a sleigh, and in addition to the regular uniform and greatcoat each wore long woollen drawers and stockings, loose moccasins filled with straw, a flannel shirt, a thick sweater, a chamois jacket, a fur cap and gauntlets and a woollen scarf. Each man was issued two blankets, one of which was partially sewn to form a blanket sack. Two sheepskin coats or buffalo robes were provided per sleigh. The journey from Woodstock, 185 miles, took six days. Troops coming from St. John travelled the entire distance, 319 miles, in sleighs over a period of ten days. From Riviére du Loupe the troops were taken by rail to their various posts. The whole affair was clearly illustrative of the tenuous state of winter communications between Canada and Great Britain.

During the first ten weeks of 1862, 6,823 British regulars landed in New Brunswick and were transported by sleigh. In all, nearly 18,000 regulars were on active service in Canada, including two battalions of Guards (1st Bn. Grenadier Guards and 2nd Bn. Scots Fusilier Guards), who seldom serve overseas except in extreme emergency. Arrangements had also been made to send to Canada 30,000 arms complete with accoutrements. This shipment consisted of pattern 1858 Enfield long and short rifles, and artillery and cavalry carbines.

Two Militia Acts were passed in 1863; their effect was to increase the Volunteer Militia to 35,000, and to establish schools of instruction for officers. The distinction between Class A and Class B of the Active Militia was abolished so that all would now serve without pay; uniforms, however, would be provided.

In 1863 the infantry and artillery were issued with new uniforms of British manufacture. Up to this point infantry corps had been clothed as Rifles in dark green uniforms. Henceforth most infantry units were clothed as Infantry of the Line, in scarlet with blue facings. The tunic was similar, in most respects, to the British 1856 pattern; but cuffs differed in being decorated with an Austrian knot—silver cord traced with Russia braid for officers, and white cord for other ranks. Uniform buttons were of white metal (silver-plated for officers), bearing a beaver within a circlet inscribed 'Canada Militia', the circlet surrounded by maple leaves and surmounted by a crown. A second order was placed in 1866, and these uniforms came with brass buttons of the above pattern. Several of the other ranks' tunics had cloth shoulder straps instead of cords.

Trousers were of Oxford mixture. Headdress was the 1861 pattern quilted shako or the undress Kilmarnock cap. Accoutrements consisted of a white buff waist belt with a universal locket bearing only the crown, expense pouch, bayonet frog, cap pouch and cartridge box strap with a black cartridge box. Rifle accoutrements were all black. Greatcoats and knapsacks were only issued for active service. The artillery

Trooper W. J. Cunningham, The Royal Guides, No. 4 Troop, Montreal Volunteer Cavalry, 1863. Dark blue pillbox cap, stable jacket and breeches; white collar, cuffs and shoulder straps; double white stripes on pillbox and side seams of breeches; tan leather pouch, pouch belt, and sword slings; white metal buttons; black leather boots with steel spurs. A non-regulation watch chain hangs from the third button. This was very much a 'gentlemen's regiment', mainly filled with members of the Montreal Hunt Club. (Notman Collection)

uniform was similar to that worn by the Royal Artillery. In 1866 a scarlet serge Norfolk jacket, with pleated front, saw limited issue, but proved to be very unpopular. The 1863 pattern Canadian uniforms remained in use until circa 1870 when replaced, for infantry, by uniforms based on the British 1868 pattern.

Border skirmishing

During the Civil War Canada was a hive of activity, with Confederate agents working out of several cities. Their escapades eventually became a thorn in Canada's side and turned popular opinion against the South, while causing further ill-feeling between Canada and the United States.

These activities culminated in the St. Albans, Vermont, raid in 1864. Capt. George Conger, US Army, organized a body of local inhabitants who fired upon the raiders. In the ensuing firefight one raider was killed, one of Conger's group was killed and two wounded. Needless to say, all this angered the Americans no end, not to mention panicking the border states, which now feared a Confederate threat from the north; neither were Canadians impressed with this outright breach of their neutrality.

When the United States moved to abrogate the

Reciprocity Treaty between Canada and the USA, Canada's Governor General, Lord Monk, took steps to end further Confederate action in Canada. Two thousand volunteers were called out for duty at various points along the border. A secret police force was established, and tasked with preventing further breaches of Canadian neutrality, including the volunteering of Canadians for service in the US Army.

It is estimated that no less than 20,000 British North Americans, and possibly as many as 50,000, served in the US Army during the Civil War. Of these 28 were awarded the Medal of Honor; and four—Henry Benham, Jacob Cox, John Farnsworth and John McNeil—attained general's rank. Many British North Americans also served in the Confederate army, although just how many is not known.

The threat of war with the United States had clearly illustrated to the British North American colonies the importance of political union for their mutual defence, and was one of the causes which led to the union of the provinces of Canada, New Brunswick and Nova Scotia in 1867 as the Dominion of Canada.

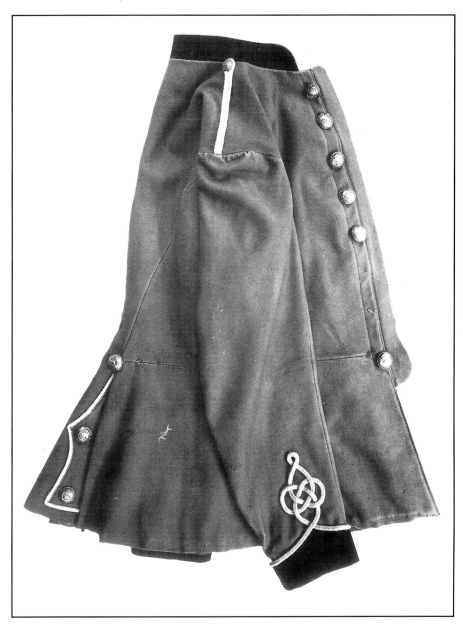

Canadian Militia other ranks' tunic issued in 1863: scarlet with dark blue collar and cuffs; white metal buttons, a beaver surrounded by a 'Canada Militia' riband, and an oak wreath; white worsted braid and cord shoulder straps (changed to blue cloth in 1866). (RCMP Museum Collection)

Undress uniform worn by Captain Stephen Catley, 13th Battalion of Infantry, Hamilton, Ontario, 1862–67, including service during the Fenian Raids of 1866. Coarse scarlet serge with collar and cuffs in dark blue, with silver lace of the same quality as the 1856 pattern full dress tunic; silver buttons, a crowned VR within a laurel wreath; silver Canada Militia belt plate, with a crown over a beaver; dark blue forage cap with scarlet band. An interesting variant of undress uniform of similar cut to the other ranks' frock. (From the Glenbow Museum, formerly in the RUSI Collection)

THE FENIAN RAIDS, 1866 & 1870

No sooner had the American Civil War drawn to a close than a new threat materialized south of the border. The Fenian Brotherhood, the American branch of the Irish Republican Army, was formed in New York City in 1858. The Brotherhood's primary goal was Irish independence; this they would attempt to achieve by an invasion of Canada. However, the Fenian ranks were infiltrated by British and Canadian agents who kept the government well apprised of their activities.

On 7 March 1866, anticipating trouble on St. Patrick's Day, 10,000 Volunteer Militiamen were

placed on active service under the command of Lt. Gen. Sir John Michel, commanding Her Majesty's forces in North America. St. Patrick's Day passed without serious incident.

As it was not possible to keep a large number of volunteers on active service indefinitely the frontier was, to a great extent, unguarded when the Fenians finally moved. Their first foray, directed against Campobello Island in Passamaquoddy Bay, achieved nothing. On the Niagara frontier the threat was more serious. The plan entailed three widely spaced attacks: from Chicago against Western Ontario; from Buffalo and Rochester over the Niagara River; and from New York and the Atlantic seaboard cities north along the Lake Champlain route into Canada East. Only the raids across the Niagara River and north along the Lake Champlain route materialized.

On 27 May 1866 Col. John O'Neill and his 13th Fenian Regiment moved by train north out of Nashville, Tennessee, arriving in Buffalo, New York, on the 29th with reinforcements gathered en route. By 31 May approximately 1,500 troops had concentrated in Buffalo. Canadian authorities were hesitant to respond because of previous false alarms; but on 31 May the Adjutant General was instructed to call out 14,000 volunteers. On 2 June the remainder of the volunteer force was called out so that by the 3rd 20,000 men were under arms.

In the meantime O'Neill, who had taken command of the Fenian forces when the expedition leader failed to arrive, marched out of Buffalo to Lower Black

▲ *General issue other ranks' brass belt plate, Canadian Volunteer Militia in the 1860s, shown here on a rifle unit's blackened buff leather belt. (Parks Canada Collection)*

▶ *Gilt belt plate of Captain S. Catley, 13th Battalion of Infantry, 1866. This pattern was in general use for officers, though some units had their title in place of 'Canada Militia'. The beaver was a popular national symbol of the day. (Glenbow Museum Collection)*

Rock. On the night of 31 May/1 June he and about 800 of his followers crossed the Niagara River in two steamboats and four canal barges, landing at Fort Erie in the Niagara Peninsula.

Recognizing that the Welland Canal and a parallel railway line were the likely Fenian objective, Gen. Napier, commanding Canada West, concentrated forces at both its northern and southern ends. To the south, at Port Colborne, was Lt. Col. Alfred Booker's force of 850 men of the 2nd Bn. Queen's Own Rifles, 13th Bn. of Infantry (Hamilton), and the York and Caledonia Rifle Companies. To the north, at St. Catherine's, were Col. George Peacocke's 16th Regt., three companies of the 47th Regt. and a detachment of artillery. He was later joined by the 10th Royal Regt., the Lincoln Militia, two more companies of regulars, and the Governor General's Body Guard. This force numbered about 1,700 men. Col. Peacocke was in overall command of the two forces.

Booker's instructions were to rendezvous with Peacocke at Stevensville (via Ridgeway), about midway between them; from there the combined force would move against the Fenians. In addition, orders called for a detachment of gunners to board a steamer at Port Colborne and patrol the Niagara River from Fort Erie to Chippawa. Then Booker received intelligence that the Fenian force had moved from Fort Erie. Without Col. Peacocke's knowledge a new plan was developed: the steam vessel would sail to Fort Erie to cut off the Fenian escape while Booker's force moved overland by train to occupy the town. The Fenians would be trapped.

At 3:30 a.m. on 2 June Col. Peacocke received a telegram informing him of the plan. He did not approve, and ordered the original plan to be carried out.

At nightfall on 1 June O'Neill's Fenians advanced further up the Niagara River towards Ridge Road. In

The 5th Royal Light Infantry of Montreal, c. 1865. Officer (lying in front) and staff sergeant (standing) wear the 1856 pattern tunic, two corporals the 1863 pattern tunic with the white Austrian knot cuff. All tunics are scarlet with dark blue facings, white braid and white metal buttons (silver for the officer). Note the Kilmarnock cap, the quilted pattern shakos, and the sword worn by the staff sergeant. (Parks Canada)

▲ Ensign, 26th Middlesex Battalion of Infantry, Strathroy, Ontario, c.1866. He wears the new pattern of officer's tunic, introduced to the militia in 1863: scarlet with silver lace, braid and buttons, white piping, and single crimson shoulder strap. This replaced the 1856 pattern, had only a brief life, as the militia adopted the British 1868 pattern soon after its appearance. (NAC photo c.52331)

▶ Sergeant Robert William Bell, No. 5 Coy, 41st Brockville Battalion of Rifles in marching order, c.1866. Rifle green (black) frock tunic with scarlet, black-braided collar; scarlet backing to black sergeant's chevrons. Black leather equipment with greatcoat strapped to the pack; short Snider-Enfield rifle with sword bayonet. Note the generic Rifles bugle-horn cap badge, and his collar stock. (NAC photo 29317)

the early hours of 2 June O'Neill learned of the forces mobilizing against him. At 3 a.m. he resumed his march, now heading south toward Ridgeway. His forces, which now numbered barely 500, occupied positions on Limestone Ridge about one and a half miles north of Ridgeway.

Col. Booker, his troops loaded in box cars, proceeded to carry out the original plan. Upon detraining at Ridgeway Booker was informed by some local farmers that the Fenians were at hand. This information he chose to disregard, as Peacocke's last

communication had definitely stated that the Fenians were at Frenchman's Creek. Booker began the advance up Ridge Road toward Stevensville at 6:30 a.m. Unfortunately, no one had arranged transportation for the reserve ammunition. No. 5 Company, Queen's Own Rifles, formed the advance guard 1,000 yards ahead of the main body. The previous day their Enfields had been replaced with Spencer repeating rifles.

As the Canadian advance guard approached Garrison Road, two Canadian Government detectives approached on horseback bearing news that the Fenians were right behind. Soon after crossing Garrison Road, some time after 7 a.m., the advance guard came under fire, dashed for cover and began to return fire. Lt. Col. Gillmore, commanding the 2nd

Albert Edward, Prince of Wales (3rd from right), in the uniform of an unattached lieutenant-colonel, at Charlottetown, PEI, in July 1860 during his tour of Canada. The prince's visit was a great personal success and gave considerable encouragement to recruiting for the budding volunteer movement. The prince is posed with his staff and the Lieutenant Governor. It is perhaps sartorially significant that everyone is in either civil or military uniform. (NAC photo c.1271)

Bn., deployed the remainder of his battalion. Numbers 1 and 2 Companies were moved up into line with No. 5 Company, to the left and right respectively, with Numbers 3 and 4 Companies in support. Number 6 Company was ordered to flank the enemy from the right while No. 7 Company, supported by No. 8, were to attempt the same on the left. Numbers 9 and 10 Companies remained in reserve. Then came the news that Peacocke would be delayed.

During the night he had received militia reinforcements who now refused to move until they had eaten breakfast. To this Peacocke conceded, having no idea that Booker's column was marching directly for the Fenian position.

However, it appeared that the regulars would not be needed. An hour had passed and the Canadian line

Colour-Sergeant I. S. Henderson, 3rd Battalion Victoria Volunteer Rifles of Montreal, 1866, in marching order. Rifle green undress tunic, with scarlet collar and cuffs trimmed with black braid. Although the Snider-Enfield rifle was in general issue by this time, he is still armed with the muzzle-loading Enfield with the long sword bayonet. All equipment is black leather. Note that the cap and ammunition pouches are worn on the waist belt. (Notman Collection)

had cautiously advanced a half-mile to the Fenian skirmish line along Bertie Road. By now the Queen's Own were running low of ammunition. Three fresh companies of the 13th Battalion and the York Rifle Company were rushed forward to relieve Numbers 1, 2 and 5 Companies before continuing the advance.

As the advance was pressed the Fenians' front line began to falter, the panic spreading to the main body. O'Neill, accompanied by some of his officers, rode forward to rally the men. Then at about 9:30 a.m. came shouts of 'Cavalry!', when some of the militiamen spotted a few mounted Fenians in the bushes.

Booker ordered 'Prepare for Cavalry', and five companies of the Queen's Own formed square on Ridge Road. The Fenians, of course, had no cavalry: about to retire from the field, they looked on in disbelief at the manoeuvre which had just been executed—the Canadian square provided the best target they had had all day. All thought of retreat disappeared, and the Fenians began to pour fire into the square. Realizing what he had done, Booker ordered 'Extend, Reform Column'. Numbers 1 and 2 Companies did so, but the remainder stayed in position.

Gillmore then ordered the 'Retire' to be sounded; the Queen's Own turned about and began to march back. As they approached the unengaged companies of the 13th Battalion these panicked and broke ranks. Then to their rear the Queen's Own heard the forward companies of the 13th racing back. Enough was enough— all ran for the rear. After about 200 yards the mad rush became a walk, but nothing could stop the retreat. Booker's Column suffered nine killed, 32 wounded and six prisoners, not including seven cases of sunstroke and exhaustion and three died of disease. Fortunately the Fenian pursuit was pressed only as far as Ridgeway, the main body halting on the battlefield to collect souvenirs. Within a few hours O'Neill had his men on the march back to Fort Erie.

In the meantime, at Fort Erie, 76 men of the Welland Canal Field Battery and the Dunville Naval Brigade were landed by the steam tug *W. T. Robb*, and proceeded to round up Fenian stragglers. At about 2 p.m., much to their surprise, the Fenian main body arrived, and their advance guard opened fire on the Canadians. Most of the Naval Brigade were picked up by the *W. T. Robb*, but the Welland Battery

Major-General Sir Hastings Doyle, KCMG, Commanding British Troops in N. America, 1870 (he commanded the British garrison in Halifax 1861–67). He is in full dress: scarlet tunic with gold lace and single twisted cord shoulder strap; gold and crimson sash and sword belt with gilt fittings; dark blue trousers with gold stripes; dark blue greatcoat with black velvet collar; mameluke hilt sword; white-over-red plume on gold-laced cocked hat. This tunic was replaced in 1880 by a pattern with oakleaf-embroidered collar and cuffs, and the sash moved to the waist at the same time. (Notman Collection)

stayed and fought. The fighting, at close quarters, was spirited and bloody, but the Canadians were finally overrun by superior numbers. Casualties amounted to six wounded and 36 prisoners; the Fenians suffered four killed, five mortally wounded and 14 wounded.

After pondering the situation, O'Neill re-embarked his troops for the return to Buffalo. The gunboat USS *Michigan* was waiting, took the Fenian barge in tow, and placed its passengers under arrest.

The Fenians were not quite finished. At St. Armand, near Missisquoi Bay, Canada East, were stationed four companies of untrained border volunteers under the command of Capt. W. W. Carter, 16th Regiment. On the afternoon of 4 June came news that a force of Fenians was mobilizing and would attack that evening. Not wishing to expose his raw troops, he felt obliged to fall back on a supporting force at St. Jean. The frontier was now wide open. His action was premature, and he was later severely reprimanded.

On 7 June a force of 500 to 1,000 Fenians (accounts vary) under command of Brig. Gen. Samuel Spier crossed the frontier following the Lake Champlain route. They occupied positions at Pigeon Hill, Cooks Corners, St. Armand, Frelighsburg and Stanbridge. The force dispatched to deal with the incursion comprised the Prince Consort's Own Rifle Brigade, 25th Regt., 7th Regt., the Royal Guides, the border volunteers, and No. 2 Field Battery (Hochelaga). On the afternoon of the 9th the force arrived at St. Armand only to find it deserted. Moving on to Pigeon's Hill, the Royal Guides encountered a party of approximately 200 Fenians returning to the

Major-General Hon. James Lindsay commanded the Brigade of Guards in Canada in 1862, and the troops stationed in Canada East in 1866. He was appointed to wind down the British garrison in Canada, and responsible for the Red River Expedition (KCMG); it was Lindsay who appointed Wolseley to command the column. He wears in this 1870 photo the general officer's pattern gold and crimson sash, dark blue frock coat with black velvet collar and cuffs, and dark blue overalls with leather bootings. With him is his ADC, Capt. William Julius Gasgoine, in staff pattern frock coat, scarlet vest, white glazed leather pouch belt (only ADCs of field rank wore gold lace staff pattern) and cocked hat (on table). Gascoigne was later GOC Canadian Militia 1895–98, and GOC Hong Kong during the Boxer Rebellion of 1900. (Notman Collection)

Lieutenant-General Sir Charles Windham, KCB, 1868; he commanded the British troops in N. America from 1867 until his death in early 1870. Here he is wearing the 1857 pattern general officer's full dress: scarlet tunic with dark blue collar and cuffs, gold lace, Queen's crown rank badge on collar; gold sash with crimson stripes. The wearing of medals had not yet been codified, and personal whim prevailed as may be seen here. His sword belt and slings are scarlet and gold round cord, a pattern often seen with presentation swords. (Notman Collection)

border; the Guides charged, killing several and taking 16 prisoners. In the meantime the Rifle Brigade moved in from the north, and a half-battery of Armstrong guns were deployed on the crest of Pigeon's Hill. The 25th were held in reserve. Only the Royal Guides were engaged.

On 22 June a small body of Fenians returned to Pigeon's Hill, fired with no effect on the 21st Bn. (Richelieu Light Infantry), then fled. For now the Fenians had had enough.

To all this the militia had responded as well as might be expected; but there had been mistakes. Field Marshal Wolseley later reflected that ... 'the Canadians are a splendid race of men and they make first rate soldiers; but officers accustomed to command, or who were even instructed in the art of commanding, were then few. This is the weak side of all militia forces that are rarely assembled for instruction, but it is difficult to convince the officers themselves of this fact.' As to staff work, little provision had been made to sustain a force on active service. Most of the militia went without rations or the haversacks in which to carry them, and water-bottles were in short supply. Camp equipment was nowhere to be found and medical supplies were inadequate.

When, in early 1866, the Fenian threat became apparent, the regulars and militia were still armed with muzzle-loading Enfield rifles. When reports indicated that some of the Fenians were armed with Spencer repeating rifles an alarmed Canadian Government took action. In March a purchase of 300 Spencer rifles, model 1865 of .56–50 rimfire calibre, was authorized, and additional orders followed; some of these were on hand before the end of the month. As mentioned, some of these weapons were issued to No. 5 Company, Queen's Own Rifles, but most militiamen retained their Enfield rifles. Those Spencers issued remained in service until late 1867.

On 20 September 1866 a contract was placed with the Providence Tool Company for .50 calibre Peabody rifles with 'angular' bayonets. Three thousand rifles were delivered between 21 March and 29 April 1867, and were issued on a very limited scale. By late 1866 the entire Volunteer Militia cavalry had been armed with Spencer carbines, which they retained until replaced with Snider-Enfield cavalry carbines in 1872. A few artillery units were also issued

▶ *Lieutenant-Colonel Garnet Wolseley, aged 29, as Assistant Quartermaster General in Canada, Montreal 1862, in Staff winter uniform, including beaded moccasins and leather gaiters. So far in his hectic career he had been wounded four times and had seen action in Burma, the Crimea, the Indian Mutiny and in China. He made the most of his nine years on the Staff in Canada, studying the development of modern warfare in the nearby US Civil War; meeting General Lee; writing* The Soldier's Pocket Book *and the* Narrative of the War in China, 1860. *He saw service during the Fenian Raids, and most importantly, exercised his own independent command of the Red River Expedition in 1870, for which he received the KCMG. The nucleus of the 'Ring'— Redvers Buller, John McNeill and William Butler—served under him here. He returned to England with his reputation made. (Notman Collection)*

▲ *Major-General Bissett, CB, in the newly prescribed Mess Kit for general officers; Montreal, 1869. Scarlet jacket and vest with gold lace and braid; dark blue trousers with gold lace stripes. (Notman Collection)*

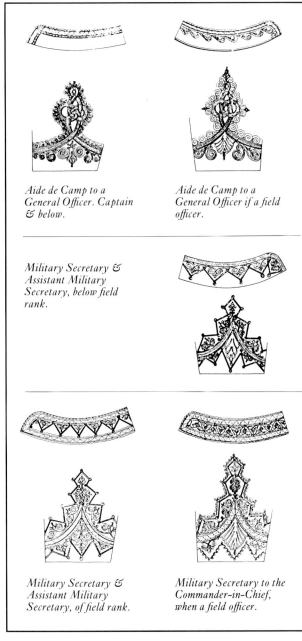

Aide de Camp to a General Officer. Captain & below.

Aide de Camp to a General Officer if a field officer.

Military Secretary & Assistant Military Secretary, below field rank.

Military Secretary & Assistant Military Secretary, of field rank.

Military Secretary to the Commander-in-Chief, when a field officer.

Lieutenant-Colonel William Earle, Grenadier Guards, in the full dress Staff uniform of his appointment as Military Secretary to Lieutenant-General Sir Charles Windham, commanding the forces in British North America. This Notman photo taken in 1867 shows the vandyke pattern of sleeve and collar lace particular to Military Secretaries.

with Spencer carbines. Also purchased in late 1866 were 250 Star carbines using a .52 calibre rimfire cartridge. During the summer of 1867, 30,000 Snider-Enfield breech-loading rifles complete with bayonets and accoutrements were received from England. These were issued to infantry, rifle and artillery units, and remained the principal arm of the militia until 1895.

On 1 July 1867 the provinces of Canada, New Brunswick and Nova Scotia were joined as the

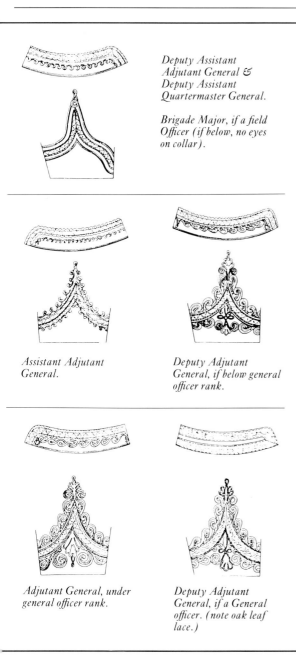

Deputy Assistant Adjutant General & Deputy Assistant Quartermaster General.

Brigade Major, if a field Officer (if below, no eyes on collar).

Assistant Adjutant General.

Deputy Adjutant General, if below general officer rank.

Adjutant General, under general officer rank.

Deputy Adjutant General, if a General officer. (note oak leaf lace.)

◀ Collar and cuff designs for the full dress Staff tunic. These show the wearer's appointment, and his rank category (general officer, field officer, or below); actual rank is indicated as usual by crowns and stars on the collar. Staff appointments with the same title could be held by officers of varying rank, depending on the size of the force to which they belonged. Based on Holding, T. H., Uniforms of the British Army etc., 1894 edition.

▼ Rear view of the full dress Staff tunic, 1856 pattern. Scarlet with dark blue collar and cuffs; gold lace and braid (silver for Canadian Militia). Glazed white leather pouch belt as prescribed for officers below field rank; black patent binocular case (referred to as a 'telescope case' in the Dress Regulations); gilt badge. This tunic, c.1860 from the PEI Museum and Heritage Foundation, is unusual in having straps on both shoulders.

Dominion of Canada; and the first Federal Militia Act was passed in 1868. It retained the conscriptive concept by retaining a reserve militia which included all able-bodied males between 18 and 60 years of age. At the same time it recognized that the Active Militia would be the mainstay of Canadian defence; accordingly, its authorized strength was raised to 40,000. Volunteers were required to serve a three-year term and could be required to drill from eight to 16 days annually. Nine military districts were established,

each commanded by a Deputy Adjutant General with the rank of lieutenant-colonel. These were further divided into the usual brigade and regimental districts and company areas.

The 1870 raid

Nothing much further was heard of the Fenians until 1870. By this time 'General' O'Neill, headquartered at Franklin, Vermont, had managed to accumulate 15,000 stand of arms and 3,000,000 rounds of

Captain J. H. F. H. Hudson, Grenadier Guards, 1869, in full dress Staff uniform as ADC to Lieutenant-General Sir Charles Windham. Scarlet tunic with dark blue collar and cuffs, gold lace and braid; dark blue trousers with gold lace seam stripes; gold-laced pouch belt. ADCs were identified by the Austrian knot figure on the cuffs, and an upright feather plume on the cocked hat. (Notman Collection)

ammunition. An attack across the Quebec border was planned for 24 May, but was postponed until the following day due to a delay in assembling troops.

On 22 May Lt. Col. W. Osborne Smith, commanding No. 5 Military District, received notice to be prepared for a raid on the frontier within his district. Information received on the 24th indicated that the Fenians were moving toward the frontier. That afternoon Osborne Smith left Montreal for St. Jean with companies of the 1st Prince of Wales' Rifles, 3rd Victoria Rifles, 5th Royal Light Infantry, 6th Hochelaga Light Infantry and the Montreal Troop of Cavalry. He also ordered Lt. Col. Brown Chamberlain to Stanbridge to assume command of the 60th Missisquoi Battalion who were mustering there. Also at Osborne Smith's suggestion, Chamberlain had telegraphed to Frelighsburg that any inhabitants with rifles who could muster before the militia should take possession of Eccles Hill.

Osborne Smith pressed on to Stanbridge Station with the Victoria Rifles and the Montreal Cavalry, having left the remainder of his force at St. Jean. On arrival at Stanbridge, some eight miles distant, Smith was informed that a small body of Missisquoi Home Guards had occupied Eccles Hill, a strong position on the immediate frontier about three miles east of Pigeon Hill. The Fenians moved to within a few hundred yards of the border and occupied a hill opposite Eccles. Chamberlain reinforced the Home Guard on Eccles Hill with a subdivision of one of his companies.

Osborne Smith then rode to Eccles Hill, where he satisfied himself that a Fenian attack was probable. Upon deciding to hold the position and after issuing instructions to Chamberlain regarding its occupation, he left for Stanbridge to hurry forward reinforcements; Lt. Col. Chamberlain, as senior officer present, was left in command of the forces on Eccles Hill. When about two miles from Stanbridge Osborne Smith was overtaken by a messenger from Chamberlain: the Fenian attack had commenced. Capt. Gascoigne continued on to Stanbridge to bring up reinforcements, while Lt. Col. Osborne Smith rode back to Eccles Hill.

The Fenian force, estimated at 350 to 400 men, advanced in close column consisting of three divisions: an advance guard moving 50 to 100 yards in front of the main body and a reserve. As the column

1: Brigade Major, Canadian Militia, 1868
2: Col. Garnet Wolseley, Assistant Quartermaster General, 1864
3: Sir Pascal-Etienne Taché ADC to the Queen, 1864

A

1: Commissariat Officer, 1864
2: Officer, Military Train, 1861
3: Surgeon Major, Medical Staff, 1870

1

2

3

B

1: Lieutenant-Colonel, Grenadier Guards, 1862
2: Bandmaster, 47th Regiment, 1863
3: Paymaster, 78th Highlanders, 1869

C

1: Sergeant, 78th Highlanders, 1868
2: Lieutenant, Rifle Brigade, 1870
3: Officer, 60th KRRC, 1868

D

1: Fenian private, 1870
2: Lieutenant-Colonel, Saint John Volunteer Battalion, 1866
3: Private, 46th (East Durham) Battalion of Infantry, 1865

E

1: Lieutenant, Royal Guides, 1862
2: Lieutenant, No. 1 Troop, Montreal Volunteer Cavalry, 1865
3: Ensign, 1st Provisional Battalion, 1865

F

1: Lt.Col., Westmoreland County Militia, 1865
2: Rifleman, 3rd Victoria Rifles, 1865
3: Quartermaster, Royal Light Infantry, 1863

G

1: Private, 22nd Battalion, Oxford Rifles, 1865
2: Captain, 3rd Victoria Rifles, 1866
3: Brigade Major, Canadian Militia, 1863

H

approached the border it advanced at the double. As soon as the advance guard crossed, Chamberlain's men opened fire. The Fenian main body returned fire from within the United States, while the advance guard scurried for cover behind barns and under a bridge. The main body halted, wavered under the Canadian fire, then broke. Some sought cover behind houses and a stone fence, while others made their way to a wood atop a hill about 250 yards from the extreme front of the Canadian line.

At this point Lt. Col. Osborne Smith arrived and took command. At 2 p.m. the Montreal Troop of Cavalry, a company of the 3rd Victoria Rifles and another detachment of the 60th Battalion arrived; with these forces Osborne Smith strengthened his skirmish line and secured his right flank. By 5 p.m. the Fenian fire had slackened; then, at 5:45, came news that the Fenians were moving a field gun into position. This Col. Osborne Smith observed about 1,200 yards to his front. The time for action was at hand. Osborne Smith ordered a rapid advance to the border in skirmishing order by the Home Guards and the 60th Battalion. The 3rd Bn. Victoria Rifles covered the advance from the right shoulder of the slope. The Fenians fled in all directions, discarding arms, accoutrements and even clothing as they ran. It was all Osborne Smith could do to restrain his troops from pursuing the Fenians across the border. By 6 p.m. it was all over.

The Canadians had not suffered a single casualty; Fenian losses were estimated at five killed and 15 to 18 wounded. Lt. Col. Osborne Smith reported that the Fenians were armed with rifles of three types: '... the United States government Springfield rifle, converted into a breech loader of ingenious construction. The Spencer and a few Springfield muzzle loaders.'

Two days later, scouts reported Fenians moving up the Trout River and crossing into Canada near

Captain Luke O'Connor, VC, 23rd Regiment (Royal Welch Fusiliers), photographed in full dress in Montreal, 1867. Scarlet tunic with dark blue facings, gilt buttons and gold lace; though it was replaced by the busby for Fusiliers in 1866, he still has the dark blue quilted shako with white plume. A colour-sergeant in 1854, O'Connor received the Crimean commission awarded to the regiment after the Alma, the VC during the Indian Mutiny, and a brevet lieutenant-colonelcy for Ashantee, retiring as Hon. Major-General and KCB. (Notman Collection)

Holbrooks Corners, Quebec. At Huntingdon were concentrated the 69th Regiment, the Beauharnois Battalion, the 50th Bn. Huntingdon Borderers, the Montreal Garrison Artillery and the Montreal Engineer Company. One Company of the 69th and seven companies of the 50th assaulted the Fenians' prepared position. The line advanced at the double with the 69th Company in the centre, flanked by companies of the 50th, firing as they moved. The 69th breached the Fenian barricade and the 50th poured through. Resistance melted as the enemy beat a hasty retreat to the border. One unfortunate Fenian was captured, while three were killed and a number wounded. The combined Canadian/British force suffered no casualties.

One of a number of group photos of NCOs and men of the 78th Highlanders taken in Montreal for Col. Lockhart in 1867. L to R, all in full dress: Drummer—white doublet with scarlet facings, his drummer's pattern claymore in a frog (no slings) on his black leather shoulder belt; Sergeant— scarlet doublet with buff facings, red and white hose; Pipe Major—dark green doublet with gold chevrons, green on green hose, black sword and dirk belts; Sergeant Major— scarlet doublet with buff facings and gold lace and chevrons. All NCO chevrons have double lace bars, changed to single in 1868. (Notman Collection)

Except for an attempted invasion of Manitoba the following year, the Fenians had seen the last of Canadian soil.

THE RED RIVER EXPEDITION 1870

As the militia mobilized to repel the Fenians, another military force was moving to the Red River Settlement. Their task: 'the maintenance of law and order' in the new Province of Manitoba.

The Hudson's Bay Company administered the Northwest Territory, which included the Settlement. Its inhabitants were mainly of mixed Indian and European blood (French, English and Scottish). An agreement was finally reached whereby sovereignty of the Northwest would be transferred, through the British Government, to the Dominion of Canada. Unfortunately nobody bothered to consult the loyal inhabitants of Red River, who feared for their land rights and culture.

The newly appointed Lieutenant Governor was refused entry to the Territory, and subsequently the French mixed-bloods (Métis) occupied Upper Fort Garry, the Hudson's Bay Company post. A Provisional Government, soon headed by Louis Riel, was

▶ *Surgeon-Major Young, 1st Battalion, 60th Rifles, 1868; Young served on the Red River Expedition as Principal Medical Officer, and is seen here in full dress uniform with British and Turkish Crimea and Indian Mutiny medals. Medical officers in this regiment wore the same pouch belt as combatant officers. (Notman Collection)*

◀ *Men of the Scots Fusilier Guards off-duty in Montreal c.1865, with an officer in frock coat. An interesting glimpse of work clothing: the white Guernseys, and the blue boat-neck sweaters of the pattern worn by Royal Navy sailors, would be needed in the autumn climate of Montreal. (Notman Collection)*

formed to negotiate the terms of entry into the Canadian Confederation. Throughout the winter the 'Canadian Party', which wanted to open the North-west to settlement, vied for control. Then Riel blundered: he court-martialled and executed an Ontario Orangeman, Thomas Scott. This enraged Orangemen in Ontario.

The Canadian Government continued to negotiate with representatives of the Provisional Government, but for Riel there would be no amnesty. In 1870 the Province of Manitoba was created and the government recognized the rights of the people of Red River. It also dispatched a military force to exert its sovereignty. While touted as not being a punitive expedition, many bent on avenging Scott's death were among the members of the Red River Expeditionary Force.

Lt. Gen. Sir James Lindsay, Commander of the British forces in Canada, lost no time in appointing the commander of the force—Col. Garnet J. Wolseley, then Deputy Quartermaster General in Canada. The British Government agreed to a joint expedition on the condition that three-quarters of the force would be Canadian and three-quarters of the cost be borne by the Dominion.

The force was composed as follows:
Detachment of Royal Artillery (Lt. Alleyne)
Detachment of Royal Engineers (Lt. Heneage)
Seven coys. of 1st Bn. 60th Rifles (Col. Fieldon)
Detachment Army Hospital Corps and Army
Service Corps (Assistant Controller Irving)
Battalion of Militia (Lt. Col. Jarvis, DAG Militia, 3rd District)
Battalion of Militia (Lt. Col. Casault, DAG Militia, 7th District)

The Canadian component of the force consisted of two Rifle Battalions: the 1st Ontario and 2nd Quebec, raised specifically for the expedition from the military districts comprising those provinces. The battalions were organized on a seven-company basis, each consisting of 50 non-commissioned officers and men, one captain, one lieutenant and one ensign. The staff of each battalion comprised one lieutenant-colonel, one major, an adjutant with rank of captain, one paymaster, one quarter-master sergeant, one hospital sergeant, one surgeon, one sergeant-major, one armourer sergeant, and one paymaster's clerk. Thus the establishment of each battalion was 382.

Assistant Surgeon Wade, 78th Highlanders, in full dress, 1869. Scarlet doublet with buff facings; ranking as a lieutenant, Mr Wade wears a crown, and has lace only along the top of his collar. In place of the combatant officer's shoulder belt with slings he wears the Medical Staff pattern pouch belt of black morocco with three lines of gold wire embroidery; Medical Staff pattern slings are attached to the regimental pattern dirk belt. (Notman Collection)

British and Canadian troops were supplied from their respective stores, and were equipped as follows:

Personal Equipment

1 knapsack	1 greatcoat
1 haversack	1 forage cap with white
1 tin plate	covering and peak front
1 waterbottle	and rear
1 mug	1 pair of ankle boots
2 blankets	1 pair of beef boots
1 waterproof sheet	1 serge blouse
1 tunic	1 pair serge trousers
1 pair of trousers	1 mosquito net
1 clasp knife	

Kit

1 cholera belt	1 holdall
1 linen bandage	1 brush for each man of
2 flannel shirts	different kinds
2 pair of socks	1 comb
1 pair of braces	1 piece of soap
2 linen shirts	2 darning needles
1 knife, fork and spoon	1 hank of thread
	2 ordinary needles

Additional for Winter

1 tunic and pair of cloth	2 knitted undershirts
trousers	2 pairs of knitted drawers
1 seal skin cap	1 muffler
1 pair mitts	

British Army greatcoat of the 1860s with Royal Engineers' insignia: blue with red piping on the shoulder and waist straps. Sergeants and below wore their chevrons on the cape as shown, senior NCOs five inches above the cuff. All NCO rank badges were yellow. (NAC photo c.17281)

Each man was armed with a short Snider-Enfield rifle with sword bayonet and accoutrements complete, and 60 rounds of service ammunition. The officers were armed with breech-loading carbines and also carried 60 rounds of ammunition. 'In addition to this weapon the regimental officers were allowed to carry any others they chose, except swords; and on the day of their departure, appeared with their persons profusely decorated with revolvers and deadly-looking scalping-knives.'[1]

The expedition assembled at Toronto in May. From there it moved by rail to the port of Collingwood on Georgian Bay, thence by steamer to Sault Ste. Marie. The canal at Sault Ste. Marie joins Lake Huron with Lake Superior; it was under American control, and they would not permit the passage of troops and war material. This problem was overcome by marching the troops through Canadian territory to the end of the canal where they re-embarked on the same vessels. Once through the Sault, the force sailed to Prince Arthur's Landing on the north-west shore of Lake Superior. Thus the first leg of the journey, 628 miles, was completed with relative ease. The remaining 500 miles would be arduous.

From his base of operations at Prince Arthur's Landing Col. Wolseley at first intended to move his force, their boats and supplies by road some 47 miles to Shebandowan Lake. The Public Works Department were to have the road ready by 1 June. On 25 May, when Col. Wolseley arrived, only 28 miles were passable for wheeled transport. Fatigue parties extended the road, but time was running short.

Upon discovering a navigable water route, up the Kaministiquia and Matawin Rivers to Shebandowan Lake, the boats were taken by that route. The stores were moved by road some 27 miles to Matawin

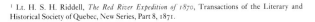

[1] Lt. H. S. H. Riddell, *The Red River Expedition of 1870*, Transactions of the Literary and Historical Society of Quebec, New Series, Part 8, 1871.

Bridge and then by road and river the remaining distance to Shebandowan Lake.

On 16 July the first detachment set out on Shebandowan Lake. The force moved in brigades of six to seven boats, each carrying ten or 11 men and 60 days' provisions, an arms chest to hold ten rifles and a waterproof bag containing ten cartridge pouches and belts. Two *voyageurs* accompanied each boat. The entire expedition comprised 87 officers, 1,048 men, 256 *voyageurs* and 15 guides. When on 1 August the last elements embarked, the leading brigade was already 150 miles ahead. From Shebandowan Lake the route followed Lac de Mille Lacs—Rainy Lake—Rainy River.

Wolseley reached Fort Francis on 4 August, as did Lt. William Francis Butler, 69th Regiment; Butler (later Lt. Gen., KCB) had been on an expedition of his own as Wolseley's intelligence officer. Having moved along the flank of the expedition he proceeded to Fort Garry via St. Paul, Minnesota. He provided Wolseley with the first reliable information on the state of affairs in Manitoba.

From Fort Francis the expedition moved via Rainy River, Lake of the Woods, and the Winnipeg River to Fort Alexander at the mouth of the Winnipeg River. There Wolseley halted to allow the militia battalions to close up. When they did not arrive after a half-day he pressed on, following Lake Winnipeg to the Red River and Lower Fort Garry. He reached the Lower Fort on the 23rd, accompanied by the 60th Rifles and detachments of artillery and engineers.

On leaving the Lower Fort Wolseley deployed a mounted company of the 60th on his right flank, 500 yards in advance of the boats with connecting files to the river bank. On the opposite bank of the river rode Lt. Butler with orders to keep in touch with the main body. Communications between the main body, the river, and the company on the right flank were maintained by signalmen with flags. That night they camped six miles below Upper Fort Garry. About 8 a.m. the next morning the force arrived at Point Douglas, about two miles from the fort. There they disembarked, and formed up on the left bank of the river.

The advance continued across the open prairie, the column covered by a skirmishing line. Two 7-pdr. bronze mountain guns were limbered to Red River carts, and a rear guard followed at 200 yards. In this

Lieutenant HRH Prince Arthur of Connaught, KG, third son of Queen Victoria, serving in the Rifle Brigade in Canada in 1870. Later, as Duke of Connaught, he was Governor General of Canada, 1911–16. He is wearing full dress with the Garter Star, and the recently discontinued quilted shako in Rifle green, with the bugle-horn badge of the Rifle Brigade below a crown on a black rosette, and a black ball tuft. (Notman Collection)

order Wolseley advanced around the village of Winnipeg, which he kept on his left flank, his right resting on the Assiniboine River. He then moved straight on to Fort Garry. The gates were closed and guns were mounted on the bastions, and Wolseley's command expected to be fired upon at any moment. But the fort was empty: Riel and his associates had fled on the approach of the column.

'The troops formed line outside the Fort, the Union Jack was hoisted, a royal salute fired, and three cheers given for the Queen ...'. Three days later leading elements of the militia battalions arrived.

Though not a shot had been fired, the expedition was quite an achievement: 1,400 men had traversed 1,200 miles, almost half the distance through a vast forested wilderness of lakes and rivers, without the loss of a single life. Hardships had been many: there were 47 portages along the route and boats, stores and equipment had to be manhandled over each. The portages were more difficult than those Wolseley later faced on the Nile. Neither were the elements kind; during the 13 weeks between arriving at Prince Arthur's Landing and marching into Fort Garry, it

▲ *Louis David Riel, leader of the Métis and head of the Provisional Gov ernment at the Red River Settlement in 1870.*

◀ *Canada General Service Medal (centre) with all the bars awarded—Fenian Raids 1866, Fenian Raids 1870, and Red River Expedition 1870—to Major A. G. Irvine, Quebec Battalion of Rifles, 1870; Commissioner, North West Mounted Police 1880–86. The first medal in this group is the Imperial Service Order, the third the North West Canada Medal 1885. The Canada GS medal was not authorized until 1899, after considerable lobbying by veterans, and then only awarded to the still-living survivors; 502 men received the Red River bar out of 1,214 who took part. Only 12, including Col. Wolseley, received three-bar medals. (RCMP Museum)*

rained for 45 days. The mosquitoes, too, were a great annoyance.

Lt. Gen. Lindsay was correct when he wrote: 'The mainspring of the whole movement was the Commander, Colonel Wolseley, who has shown throughout great professional ability. He has the faculty of organization, and resource in difficulty. He has served in many campaigns with distinction, and in this Expedition he has shown great aptitude for Command.'

The 1st Ontario and 2nd Quebec Rifles remained in garrison at the Upper and Lower Forts. On 29 August the 60th Rifles began the journey home. They were the last British troops to garrison Canada, with the exception of a small detachment at Halifax. The defence of the Dominion was henceforth a Canadian responsibility.

THE PLATES

A1: Brigade Major, Canadian Militia, 1868
Based on a Notman photo of Major G. d'O. D'Orsennens, Brigade Major, in Staff undress uniform, taken in Montreal in 1868. The tunic is somewhat unusual, basically a shortened version of the Staff frock coat, but obviously a practical garment for an officer who spent much of his time at a desk.

A2: Col. Garnet Wolseley, Assistant Quartermaster General, 1864
Based on a Notman photo taken in 1864 of Wolseley in the 1856 pattern full dress Staff uniform. The gold lace (for field officers) belt carries a black patent binocular case with a gilt 'VR' cypher badge. Staff officers of the Canadian Militia wore silver instead of gold lace and braid on this uniform.

A3: Sir Pascal-Étienne Taché, ADC to the Queen, 1864
Based on a Notman photo taken in 1864 of Colonel Sir Pascal-Étienne Taché, Minister of Militia, Upper Canada 1864–65, in the full dress uniform of an Aide de Camp (Militia) to Queen Victoria. He was wearing the Military General Service Medal with bar 'Chateauguay', for service in the War of 1812 with the

Lieutenant-Colonel William John Bolton, RA, Deputy Assistant Adjutant General (i.e. chief of staff) on the Red River Expedition, for which he received the CMG. In this 1870 photograph he is wearing the full dress Staff pattern uniform of a DAAG: scarlet tunic with gold lace and braid, gold-laced pouch belt and slings. His medals for the Crimea include the Legion of Honour and the Turkish Medjiddie. (Notman Collection)

5th Battalion Select Embodied Militia. A British Regular officer holding this appointment would have gold instead of silver lace and embroidery. Equerries to the Queen wore the same uniform with four loops on the cuff instead of three. No rank badges were worn on this tunic for either appointment.

B1: Commissariat Officer, 1864

Based on Notman photos of Acting Deputy Assistant Commissary General E. T. Price taken in Montreal in 1864. In this year the Regulations specified dark blue velvet facings, changed from the black of the 1857 Regulations; also a gold belt and slings and dark blue plume. Mr Price's uniform appears to be in transition: facings are blue, but his belt is black and plume white, though the slings are gold. In 1864 Deputy Assistants were to rank as captains, but Price still wears a lieutenant's crown.

B2: Officer, Military Train, 1861

Based on a Notman photo of Capt. J. A. Harris taken in Montreal in 1861. The Military Train was the successor to the Land Transport Corps raised for the Crimea in 1855, and more remotely to the Royal Wagon Train, disbanded in 1833. Formed in 1856, the Military Train became in 1869 the Army Service Corps, which retained the white facings.

B3: Surgeon Major, Medical Staff, 1870

Based on a Notman photo of Staff Surgeon Major H. F. Smith, stationed in Montreal on the Staff in 1870. The facings were of black velvet. The pouch belt supported a fold-out pouch of medical instruments (shown above), with a crowned Victoria cypher badge.

C1: Lieutenant Colonel, Grenadier Guards, 1862

Based on a Notman photo of Lt. Col. G. Higginson,

Lieutenant James Alleyne, RA, Montreal, 1864, in dark blue winter greatcoat trimmed with black astrakhan fur and black braid, with matching gauntlets. Lt. Alleyne saw service during the Fenian Raids, and accompanied Col. Wolseley on the Red River Expedition in command of the RA and RE detachments. He was one of the 12 survivors to receive the Canada General Service Medal with three bars when it was issued in 1899. (Notman Collection)

In camp en route to Fort Garry, probably at Collingwood, Ontario, during the Red River Expedition, 1870. Major James F. Mcleod, Brigade Major, seated; left, Staff Sergeant Douglas; right, Major Griffiths Wainewright, and Capt. and Adjutant W. J. B. Parsons (late 4/60th Rifles) of the 1st (or Ontario) Battalion of Rifles. One of the very few photos of the Expedition. (Glenbow Museum)

At present on display at Lower Fort Garry National Historic Site, this sword, with gilt scabbard and hilt and carved ivory grips, is inscribed: 'This Sword is presented by the Officers and Privates of the 1st Ontario Battalion of Rifles to Colonel Garnet J. Wolseley, as a token of their high esteem of him as an Officer and a Gentleman during the Red River Expedition'. (Parks

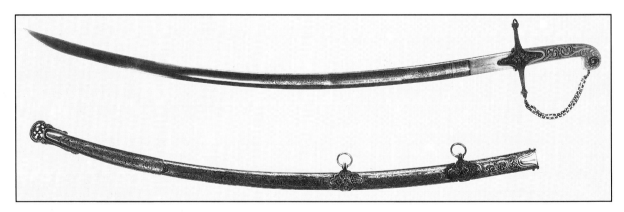

Grenadier Guards (later General, GCB, Constable of the Tower), in winter dress in Montreal in 1862. His cap may be a forage cap with a removable Persian lamb fur cover, but is possibly a specially made winter version. The greatcoat with its low pockets and Persian lamb collar (and lining?) appears to be a Grenadier pattern. Medal ribbons worn on this greatcoat may indicate that it was classed as a winter frockcoat. Note that it fastens with loops.

C2: Bandmaster, 47th Regiment, 1863
Based on a Notman photo of Bandmaster Thomas Boxall, 47th (Loyal North Lancashire) Regiment, Montreal, 1863. As with other regiments with white

Portava near the Kakabeka Falls on the route to Fort Garry, showing how the boats had to be hauled from the start of the rapids on log rollers up a hill, and overland to calm water beyond.

as a facing colour, the 47th white band tunics were faced dark blue. Note his elegant mameluke-hilted sword with scimitar blade, and regimental device on the cross guard.

C3: Paymaster, 78th Highlanders, 1869

Based on a painting by Douglas Anderson, one of a beautiful series commissioned by Parks Canada for the re-creation of the 78th Highlanders at the Halifax Citadel National Historic Site in their uniforms of 1869. Note that the Paymaster, who was always commissioned from the ranks, had considerably lower status than other officers. This is reflected in his less elaborate full dress doublet, no gold lace around the cuff slashes or pocket flaps, white sword slings and horsehair sporran tassels instead of gold. During their stay in Canada the 78th were stationed in both Montreal and Halifax.

D1: Sergeant, 78th Highlanders, 1868

Based on a Notman studio portrait of Sgt. A. Bissett,

taken in Montreal in 1868. Snowshoeing was popular as a winter sport rather than a method of military mobility. The sergeant is wearing hide moccasins over socks into which his trews are tucked.

D2: Lieutenant, Rifle Brigade, 1870

Based on a Notman photo of Lt. H. J. Fitzroy, Rifle Brigade, taken in Montreal in 1870, wearing a regimental pattern winter greatcoat. This could be worn with the lapels turned back, as shown, to form a plastron, or folded across for greater warmth.

D3: Officer, 60th KRRC, 1868

Based on Notman photographs of Lt. H. F. Eaton, 60th Rifles, taken in Montreal in 1868. Lined winter boots, fur gauntlets and Persian lamb cap were all needed in the severe cold of the Montreal winter.

Col. Wolseley's tent at Prince Arthur's Landing on Thunder Bay, 1870, en route to Fort Garry on the Red River Expedition. It is interesting to note that Wolseley's tent (centre) is a native style tipi, not an issue bell tent. The poles cross outside the apex, allowing better ventilation, and the round, above-ground level entrance cut down draughts. (PRO WE 107/9 No. 2)

E1: Fenian private, 1870

Based on research by Francis Back, published in the *Military Collector & Historian* (Vol. XL, #1, 1988), and on an actual tunic captured at the time and taken to England by Prince Arthur of Connaught, 60th Rifles. He presented it to the RE Institution in 1870, from whence it came to Parks Canada, Ottawa, in the 1980s.

E2: Lieutenant-Colonel, Saint John Volunteer Battalion, 1866

Based on the uniform of Lt. Col. Andrew C. Otty, CO of the battalion 1866–69, in the collection of the New Brunswick Museum, and on the New Brunswick Militia Dress Regulations of 1862. Colonels and lieutenant-colonels wore a crown above the point of the cuff, majors a star. With turn-down collar and loose cut, this tunic was designed to be a practical working uniform. By 1880, when the unit became the 62nd Battalion of Infantry, the standard infantry officer's tunic and blue Home Service helmet had been adopted.

E3: Private, 46th (East Durham) Battalion of Infantry, 1865

Based on a Parks Canada photo of a private of the

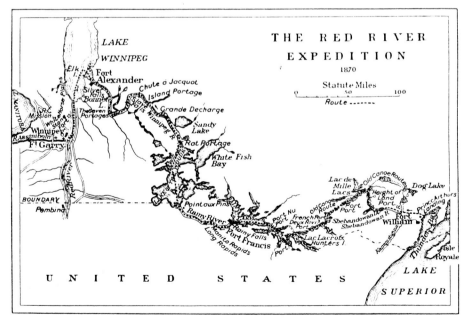

Map of the 560-mile route of the Red River Expedition from Prince Arthur's Landing to Winnipeg (the Red River settlement). They travelled by water, but broken by innumerable backbreaking overland portages, hauling their boats and carrying their cargo, in order to by-pass rapids and other impassable sections of the rivers. Before reaching Prince Arthur's Landing the troops had already travelled 628 miles from Toronto by rail, steamer and on the march. (Source: F. Maurice, Life of Lord Wolseley, 1924)

47th Battalion of Infantry in 1865. He is wearing the 1863 pattern infantry tunic, with white metal buttons with a beaver device in the centre. He carries an Enfield 1853 long pattern rifle musket with a triangular bayonet. The shako plate on his pillbox cap is unusual, but units often received their uniforms in bits and pieces probably the 46th had not yet received their quilted pattern shakos.

F1: Lieutenant, Royal Guides, 1862

Based on a Notman photo of Lt. John Pinner taken in Montreal in 1862. The Royal Guides were raised in 1862 following the *Trent* Affair, as a troop of the Montreal Volunteer Militia Cavalry. In 1866 the additional title of 'Governor General's Body Guard for Lower Canada' was granted. They saw active service during the Fenian Raids but were disbanded in 1869.

Officers of the 44th Welland Battalion of Infantry at Thorold, Ontario. This was a large training and observation camp commanded by Col. Garnet Wolseley during the summer of 1866 in response to the threat of Fenian attacks on the frontier. They wear undress dark blue tunics with black braid edging; note the turn down collar. Dark blue trousers have narrow scarlet seam stripes; and white, glazed leather sword belts are worn under the tunics. Private, at left, in 1863 pattern scarlet full dress tunic, with Kilmarnock cap.

F2: Lieutenant, No. 1 Troop, Montreal Volunteer Cavalry, 1865

Based on a Notman photograph of Lt. James Muir, taken in Montreal in 1865. As a captain, Muir commanded the troop in action against the Fenians in May 1870 at Eccles Hill. This is a good example of the Canadian penchant for adopting the most elaborate British uniforms available, in this case that of the

G1: Lieutenant-Colonel, Westmoreland County Militia, 1865

Based on the uniform of Lt. Col. Amos Botsford, CO of the unit 1832–74, New Brunswick Museum, Saint John. The top of the shako has a silver netted cap in the centre with daisy petal design in tracing braid around it. Grey was chosen by several units in the Maritime provinces in the 1860s, following the example of English volunteer regiments.

G2: Rifleman, 3rd Victoria Rifles, 1865

Based on a Notman photo of Rifleman G. Pickup, 3rd Battalion, Victoria Volunteer Rifles of Montreal, in 1865. Pictured in full marching order—which, with haversack and additional cartridge pouch on the waistbelt, must have been a considerable load—he wears the pillbox cap and undress frock. For full dress a rifle tunic and quilted pattern shako would be worn.

G3: Quartermaster, Royal Light Infantry, 1863

Based on a Notman photograph of Quartermaster. A. Robertson, Royal Light Infantry, taken in Montreal in 1862. Ranking as a first lieutenant, he has no band of lace around the top of his shako. The ball tuft is white, and his black belt and slings differentiate him from the other 'fighting' officers.

H1: Private, 22nd Battalion, Oxford Rifles, 1865

Based on a Parks Canada photo taken in the mid-1860s, this figure illustrates another of the variations of uniform worn by the Volunteer Militia. The Norfolk jacket shown was a practical, but not very smart interim garment for units which could not obtain tunics. The drummer's sword is a pleasant decorative touch for an otherwise somewhat unsmart soldier. A rural unit in Woodstock, Ontario, also known as the 22nd Battalion Volunteer Militia Rifles, it became the 3rd Battalion, Royal Canadian Regiment, in 1954. Background: drummer's sword.

H2: Captain, 3rd Victoria Rifles, 1866

Based on a Notman photo of Capt. E. A. Whitehead, 3rd Battalion, Victoria Volunteer Rifles of Montreal, wearing the quilted pattern shako in use 1861–69 with undress uniform. Note the distinctive maple leaf chain boss in place of the more common lion's head on the pouch belt, and the absence of a regimental

Private Timothy O'Hea, VC, 1st Battalion, The Prince Consort's Own Rifle Brigade. He was awarded the Victoria Cross for conspicuous bravery in putting out a fire in a railway car loaded with ammunition at Danville, between Montreal and Quebec City, on 19 June 1866. The original Warrant ruled that a VC could only be given for acts in the face of the enemy; but on 10 August 1858 a clause was added to include gallantry when not on active service. Private O'Hea's is the only Cross given under this rule. Sadly, 'he was lost in the Australian Bush (about 1876), and no trace of him could ever be found', according to a regimental history. (Regimental Museum)

Light Dragoons with the 1855 shako, with a feather, rather than the usual hair plume.

F3: Ensign, 1st Provisional Battalion, 1865

Based on Parks Canada photos of an unidentified ensign of the 1st Provisional Battalion in 1865. He is wearing a shell jacket under his greatcoat, and gaiters over ankle boots. The Provisional Battalion was made up of contingents from a number of battalions, for prolonged service on the frontier during the Fenian scares.

badge. Also shown, the Victoria Rifles badge of the 1880 pattern with the Fenian Raid battle honour of 'Eccles Hill' for the engagement on 25 May 1870, when the Fenians were driven back over the US border near St. Albans.

H3: Brigade Major, Canadian Militia, 1863

Based on a Notman photo of Maj. John McPherson, Brigade Major of Military District No. 2, Montreal, in 1863. A brigade major's Staff pattern tunic had the same cuff insignia as worn by a Deputy Assistant Adjutant General, the most junior Staff appointment. Silver braid denoted a militia officer.

A dramatic photo from the collection of the Broome County Historical Society showing 'Border Volunteers with a slain Fenian at Eccles Hill'. This all-day engagement near Montreal took place on 24 May 1870, and resulted in the invading Fenians being repulsed and retreating across the border. The two men in peaked forage caps are officers wearing the 1852 pattern double-breasted frock coat; the centre man wears a scarlet serge frock.

McPherson's collar is unusual, with its double row of lace; by regulation it should have had tracing braid at the base and a line of bullet-hole braid above. Although Canadian officers usually ordered their uniforms from London tailors, these variants do occur from time to time.

A1 Comme la plupart des personnages présentés ici, celui-ci est d'après un portrait pris par le photographe William Notman de Montreal. Cet uniforme de petite tenue a une tunique peu courante, une version plus courte de la redingote d'état-major. **A2** Uniforme complet de grande tenue d'état-major, modèle de 1856. Les officiers d'état-major de la Garde Nationale canadienne portaient une soutache d'argent à cette date. **A3** Uniforme complet de grande tenue d'un Aide de Camp (de la garde nationale) de la Reine Victoria, on ne portait pas d'écusson de rang pour cette affectation. Il a reçu sa médaille de Service général militaire pour la guerre de 1812 contre les Etats-Unis.

B1 Un uniforme de transition, apparemment, car de nouvelles ordonnances furent publiées cette année-là; il devrait avoir un ceinturon doré et un panache bleu foncé, et des écussons de rang de capitaine et non de lieutenant. **B2** Le Land Transport Corps, levé pour la guerre de Crimée en 1855, devint le Military Train l'année suivante, et en 1869 l'Army Service Corps, conservant les parement blancs. **B3** Le ceinturon à poche servait à porter une trousse d'instruments médicaux pliables.

C1 La coiffure pourrait être un expédient local, ou un bonnet de police avec housse amovible en agneau perse. La capote, avec col d'agneau perse, et peut-être aussi la doublure, est un modèle pour Granadiers, et à en juger par les rubans des médailles, était classée comme redingote d'hiver. **C2** Les régiments dont les tuniques étaient à parement blanc avaient des bandes de tunique à parements bleus foncés plutôt que rouges. Notez l'épée mamelouk. **C3** Cet uniforme reflète le grade inférieur de cet officier, toujours sorti des rangs.

D1 Notez les pantalons en tartan rentrés dans les chaussettes, les mocassins et les raquettes—les raquettes étaient un sport d'hiver populaire pour la garnison plutôt qu'une méthode sérieuse de mouvement militaire. **D2** La capote d'hiver de modèle régimentaire dont les revers se portaient croisés ou rabattus vers l'arrière, comme ici, pour former un plastron. **D3** Notez les bottes d'hiver fourrées, les gants en fourrure et le bonnet en agneau perse.

E1 D'après les recherches de Francis Back de Montreal; et d'après une tunique prise à l'ennemi et ramenée en Angleterre. **E2** Un uniforme de corvée pratique, à la coupe ample, avec col rabattu, d'après celui du Lt.Col. Otty, chef de corps de ce bataillon 1866-69. **E3** Tunique dont le modèle date de 1863; notez la plaque fixe du shako, ce qui est peu courant, sur la shako rond sans bord—les fournitures pour la Garde Nationale étaient irrégulières et les shakos n'étaient peut-être pas encore arrivés.

F1 Levée en 1862, comme troupe de la Cavalerie de la Garde Nationale Volontaire de Montreal, les Guides chargèrent en juin 1866 les Fenians lors d'un raid lancés par ces derniers à Pigeon Hill. **F2** D'après une photographie du Lt. Muir, qui prit la tête de la troupe lors du combat d'Eccles Hill en mai 1870. Cette version de l'uniforme des Dragons Légers britanniques est caractéristique du penchant de la Garde Nationale pour un costume élaboré. **F3** Cette unité fut constituée de contingents de plusieurs unités de la Garde Nationale pour le service à la frontière pendant la crise fenianne. Il porte sous sa capote une 'veste contre les obus' courte et à fond arrondi.

G1 Le gris était une couleur populaire pour les uniformes de la Garde Nationale dans les provinces maritimes pendant les années 1860, selon la mode en vogue en Angleterre. **G2** Equipement de marche complet, tunique de petite tenue et shako rond et sans bord. **G3** C'est un lieutenant, il n'y a pas de bandeau de galon sur la partie supérieure du shako; le pompon est blanc. Sa buffleterie noire le distingue des officiers combattants.

H1 Veste de style 'Norfolk', un expédient pratique mais fort peu militaire qui fut porté brièvement par la Garde Nationale Volontaire en attendant les distributions de tuniques réglementaires. Notez l'épée du tambour. **H2** Shako capitonné, modèle de 1861-69, porté avec l'uniforme de petite tenue; notez également l'écusson 'Victoria Rifles' dont le modèle est de 1880, avec distinction de bataille 'Eccles Hill', pour avoir repoussé le raid fenian le 25 mai 1870. **H3** Notez le col peu courant sur sa tunique dont le modèle est réservé à l'état-major, et dont les variations sont caractéristiques de celles trouvées parmi les officiers de la Garde Nationale canadienne.

A1 Wie die meisten Figuren stammt auch diese von einem Portraitfoto des Montrealer Fotografen William Notman. Diese Dienstuniform zeigt eine ungewöhnliche Bluse—eine verkürzte Version der Stabsjacke. **A2** Gala-Stabsuniform von 1856. Stabsoffiziere der kanadischen Miliz trugen damals silberne Borten. **A3** Gala-Uniform eines Flügeladjutanten (Miliz) von Königin Victoria—für diesen Posten gab es keine Rangabzeichen. Seine Military General Service-Medaille erhielt er für seine Beteiligung am Krieg gegen die USA 1812.

B1 Offenbar eine Art von Übergangsuniform—in diesem Jahr wurden neue Bestimmungen erlagssen; er sollte eigentlich einen goldenen Gürtel und eine dunkelblaue Feder tragen, und die Rangabzeichen eines Hauptmanns anstatt eines Leutnants. **B2** Das Land Transport Corps, aufgestellt für den Krimkrieg 1855, wurde im nächsten Jahr zur militärischen Fahrtruppe, und dann 1869 zum Army Service Corps, wobei es die weissen Aufschläge beibehielt. **B3** Der Patronengürtel trug einen zusammenklappbaren Behälter für medizinische Instrumente.

C1 Die Kopfbedeckung könnte einfach ein lokaler Notbehelf gewesen sein, oder eine Feldmütze mit einer abnehmbaren Persianerfellhülle. Der lange Mantel mit Persianerkragen—und vielleicht Persianerfutter—scheint Grenadierstil zu haben und war nach den Ordensspangen zu schliessen ein Wintermantel. **C2** Regimenter, deren Blusen weisse Aufschläge hatten, hatte dieses Regiment dunkelblaue anstatt rote Aufschläge. Siehe Mameluken-Schwert. **C3** Die Uniform zeigt den niedrigen Rang dieses Offiziers, der aus den unteren Rängen aufgestiegen war.

D1 Die engen Hosen sind unten in die Socken hineingestopft; er trägt Moccasins und Schneeschuhe—das war ein beliebter Wintersport in der Kaserne, nicht so sehr für den militärischen Einsatz. **D2** Der lange Wintermantel nach Rdgimentsmuster konnte entweder mit nach vorne zusammengeschlagenen Revers getragen werden, oder zurückgeschlagen als eine Art Plaztron. **D3** Siehe die gefütterten Winterstiefel, Pelzhandschuhe und Persianerkappe.

E1 Beruhend auf Forschungen von Francis Back aus Montreal, und auf einer Bluse, die erbeutet und nach England gebracht wurde. **E2** Eine praktische Dienstuniform, lose geschnitten, mit einem umschlagbaren Kragen, beruhend auf der von Oberstleutnant Otty, Bataillonskommandant von 1866-69. **E3** Bluse von 1863; siehe Tschakodeckel auf unübliche Weise an der Kappe befestigt—die Lieferungen für die Miliz waren unregelmässig, und die richtigen Tschakos waren vielleicht noch nicht eingetroffen.

F1 Aufgestellt 1862 als Truppe der Freiwilligen Kavalleriemiliz Montreal, war diese Einheit beim Angriff gegen die Fenian-Banden bei Pigeon Hill im Juni 1866 dabei. **F2** Nach einem Foto von Leutnant Muir, der die Truppe im Mai 1870 bei Eccles Hill befehligte. Diese Version der Uniform der britischen Leichten Dragoner war typisch für die Vorliebe der Milizen für komplexe Uniformen. **F3** Diese Einheit wurde aus Kontingenten mehrerer Milizeinheiten während der Fenian-Krise für den Grenzdienst zusammengestellt. Unter dem langen Mantel trägt er eine kurze, unten abgerundete Jacke.

G1 Grau war eine beliebte Farbe für Milizuniformen in den Küstenprovinzen während der 60er Jahre, inspiriert durch die damalige Mode in England. **G2** Volle Marschausrüstung, Feldbluse und flache runde Kappe. **G3** Er hat den Rang cincs Leutnants und kein Litzenband auf seinem Tschako; die Quaste ist weiss. Sein schwarzer Gürtel und Riemenzeug unterscheiden ihn ebenfalls von Feldoffizieren.

H1 Die Jacke im Norfolk-Stil, praktische aber unmilitärische, wurde für kurze Zeit von der Freiwilligen-Miliz getragen, die auf das Eintreffen der vorschriftsmässigen Blusen warteten. Siehe den Trommler-Degen. **H2** Der gesteppte Taschako nach dem Muster von 1861-69wurde mit der Dienstuniform getragen; siehe auch Abzeichen der Victoria Rifles von 1880, und die Kampfauszeichnung 'Eccles Hill' für die Abwehr des Fenian-Angriffs vom 25.Mai 1870. **H3** Siehe unüblichen Kragen an dieser Stabsbluse, typisch für die Variationen bei den kanadischen Milizoffizieren.